The Volume of Our Incongruity

poems by

Diane Vogel Ferri

Finishing Line Press
Georgetown, Kentucky

The Volume of Our Incongruity

Copyright © 2018 by Diane Vogel Ferri
ISBN 978-1-63534-713-5 First Edition
All rights reserved under International and Pan-American Copyright Conventions. No part of this book may be reproduced in any manner whatsoever without written permission from the publisher, except in the case of brief quotations embodied in critical articles and reviews.

ACKNOWLEDGMENTS

Many thanks to the editors of the following print and online journals in which these poems were first published:

The Summer Before College: *Rubbertop Review: Akron University*
Gray: *Common Threads*
On the Calm Side: *Common Threads*
The Burned Boy: from the chapbook *Liquid Rubies—Pudding House Press*
Punta Cana: from the chapbook *Liquid Rubies—Pudding House Press*
Mothers and Sons: *Sacred Journey*
The Boneyard: *Hessler Street Fair Anthology*

With my love and gratitude to Lou, Ryan and Kate who have been my inspiration.

With appreciation to Gail Bellamy, Lee Chilcote and Lou Suarez for their mentorship and encouragement.

Publisher: Leah Maines
Editor: Christen Kincaid
Cover Art: Glen A. Heberling
Author Photo: Lou Ferri
Cover Design: Elizabeth Maines McCleavy

Printed in the USA on acid-free paper.
Order online: www.finishinglinepress.com
also available on amazon.com

Author inquiries and mail orders:
Finishing Line Press
P. O. Box 1626
Georgetown, Kentucky 40324
U. S. A.

Table of Contents

I. That was when songs made decisions for me...

The Summer Before College 1
Gray 2
The Burned Boy 3
The Carpenter 4
Windows 5
Thirteen 6
Wading 8

II. Some nights I stand naked before you...

Geometry 10
Stalking 11
September Poem 12
A Marriage 13
Punta Cana 14
Remainder 15
The Desire 16
Wife 17
To Have Love 18
On the Calm Side 19
Where It Lived 20
There is a Last Time for Everything 21

III. A mother is thirsty woman drinking every last drop of the sea...

Grace 24
In the Waiting Room 25
Mothers and Sons 26
Bonfire 27
The Rat 28
High Tide 29
The Boneyard 30
Black Dress 31
Crawl Space 32

I.

That was when songs made decisions for me...

The Summer before College

In a colorless uniform I rode my bicycle
to the brand new Holiday Inn.
Solitary hours of changing sheets
and dusting faux surfaces,

of double-checking for a rogue hair
on the sink. I'd stare at a pair of hiking boots,
a men's magazine, a used condom
and imagine who had been there,

what they had been doing.
Silence weighed my body down
and magnified the loneliness,
so one August day I pushed a door shut,

turned on the television and sat on a bed
to watch Richard Nixon resign,
breaking the rules to witness
that singular shameful moment.

Days of laundry duty, the drone
of dryers, blinding white towels
folding when I closed my eyes at night.
The radio played *the first time ever I saw your face*

over and over and the music spun yearning
into my eighteen-year old heart.
That was when songs made decisions for me,
and at 4:00 on that same day I said
I quit.

Gray

I remember gray.
The pale neutral sky as I walked
down the street to their house
on smooth hot asphalt.

Grandpa in the back yard
picking up a heavy horseshoe
from the slate-colored clay.
The clink of ringers—iron against iron.

His graphite markings
on the basement two-by-four
carefully measured
the growth of eight grandchildren.

In the living room, Grandma
lying on the gray couch
like a pencil sketch
watching a black and white TV.

The skin of her barren head
blended in with the carpet, the sky,
the ashes in the ashtray
until we couldn't see her anymore.

The Burned Boy

in the 1962 children's ward
birthed my fear of fire.
He smiled at me with a lipless grin,
through his tiny eye-slits as we sat
among wailing voices coming from giant cribs.

The skin of his limbs was
charred deep and garnet-like,
wrinkled as a turtle's neck.
Little nose and ears diminished,
burned off, maybe ashes on the floor now.

We wiled the day away in the hospital playroom
making plaster-molded figures,
choosing children's books from
the visiting cart with my pink hands,
his elderly-looking hands.

At the end of playtime
the tiny bandaged body
would shuffle down the hall
like a wise old man,
like someone who had seen too much.

The Carpenter

We could walk through the walls
into the sweet sawdust
of the house he was building,
climb the skeleton staircase

and wave to everyone below.
Breathe the fresh-sawn planks,
touch the tiny pencil markings
from Grandpa's root-like hands.

This will be the kitchen.
This is a bedroom.

We ran between clean white
two-by-fours, shouting *you're it!*
We climbed and slid down piles
of dirt and gravel, walked the perimeter

of the muddy yard, jumped over
stacks of golden wood,
collected handfuls of crooked nails
while Grandpa lumbered

through the construction debris,
his walk more of a well-worn sway,
his cigar smoke mingling
with the wood particles in the air.

Windows

I stretched my arm to touch the back window
to be the last one out of Ohio and into the new state.

Looking out side windows without distraction
I could see the first foreign license plate,

counting farm animals, compiling lists,
our bare feet poked out of the Rambler

back window into the summer breeze.
Holding up signs—*honk if you love Jesus,*

waving to strangers, laughing at faces
in cars behind us, making up songs, pounding out

Indian chants against the front seat until
Mom and Dad had enough of that foolishness.

To California and back, to Gettysburg
monuments and graves, bloody battlefields,

to Williamsburg ladies in long, stifling
dresses and men in silly wigs and three-cornered hats.

We fought over seats, made deals for heated motel pools.
Dad would take me, the oldest, swimming after dark.

In the night travel of counting stars, watching for spaceships,
looking for God, I wrote stories and poems

sitting on the floor of the back seat behind Dad
driving us safely, safely home.

Thirteen

In the blossoming month of June
there is a tree that smells like grape bubble gum.
Its scent causes me to walk out of my adult door
right into the candy aisle
of the drug store at the top of my street.
I am thirteen

and have nothing to do but get on
my chrome and blue bicycle,
pedal the incline of Seneca Road,
lean the unlocked bike
against the hot brick wall
and enter the cool relief.

There are other kids congregated there
around the shelves of rainbow sweets,
coins bristling in their pockets.
Pink watermelon sticks can last all day,
grape bubble gum to snap, pop and blow,
enough to annoy my mother all afternoon.

The magazine aisle is a feast
of boys on glossy covers, boys out of reach,
boys in bell-bottoms and fringed vests.
And skinny girls with giant eyes in peasant dresses,
mini-skirts, clog shoes, brown suede purses
hanging off of their golden shoulders.

How I want to hold that boy's hand.
How I want to look just like Twiggy.
How my thirteen year-old hopes and dreams sizzle and grow.
The owner of the store breaks the reverie:
If you kids want to look at those magazines
you'll have to buy them.

I take my grape gum, my watermelon delights,
my shiny boy crushes to the counter
and surrender my baby-sitting money.
I glide all the way down Seneca Road
with my treasures,
with my bubble gum dreams.

Wading

Hot summer nights we'd pile
into the station wagon, three kids and a dog,

a short trip to the creek, throw off shoes and socks,
to wade on flat, black Ohio shale and skip stones,

to ungracefully fall in a swimming hole
fully clothed and laughing in the security

of parents nearby, in the innocence
of fear-free, languid summers.

Now in the Caribbean Sea
among coral reef tide pools

among clusters of multicolored sea snails, tiny fish,
sponges and porous rock formations

prehistoric birds fly above
my sun-stained skin and sun-bleached hair,

and I remember the wonder of warm feet in cool water
on a hot summer night

a world and a lifetime away
from that first wading into life.

II.

Some nights I stand naked before you...

Geometry

We
are not everything to each other,
not one of your equivalent couples.
Our lives move on a parallel continuum.
Standing stubbornly at our endpoints,
the chase around the circumference of our shared circle
lasts until one of us crosses the diameter.
The volume of our incongruity is acute;
a marriage of asymmetrical sides and angles.

But
when I am as useless as a broken protractor
you wait for me to glue myself together.
When I am being obtuse you try to understand me.
When you won't let me into your sphere of consciousness
I wait and pray in a prism of reflection,
hoping to meet at a common vertex.
We stumble along our separate line segments,
always, eventually, intersecting at a given point.

Stalking

The blue heron has been at the edge
of the pond all morning stalking fish
with surreal patience, with the stillness

of a lawn ornament or my unmoving
body lying next to yours at night.
He makes no sound, just like us.

The fish does not know that the heron
is there, even though surely it could look up
and see what is so close.

The heron crouches low, just as I am
sometimes, as we are,
half of what could be.

Then the great bird sees what it wants,
its mouth plunges into the water and pulls
out the prize that will sustain its life.

The fish does not fight the inevitable.
The heron stands proudly upright to savor
the moment before swallowing the fish whole.

September Poem
    (Things are Falling)

Everything is here but you
on this evolving September day.
The first curly leaves surround me
like sunbathers on the beach.
Overhead, green ones move like dancers
sending a strobe light of sun on my skin.

Near the whir of traveling traffic
I am sitting still with my shawl of poetry.
I hear you pounding in the garage,
smoking out your losses,
and this is how we play
the game with no winners.

A Marriage

Some days we take it down brick by brick,
that thing we built long ago.
We chip at the mortar with bare hands
scraping bits of skin off our fingers.

Some days we move as one giant shoulder
toppling ramparts with a single shove,
moving as easily as a wet embrace
in the warm waters of a hot tub.

Some nights I stand naked before you,
transparent as an empty glass.
I hand you stones to throw
but they drop from your fingers to the floor.

Some nights light comes from your tongue
to brighten my darkness and
truth flies across the bedroom ceiling
like gleaming contrails in the sky.

Some days there is no fear, no twist,
no reduction of you or me.
The reason remains, the knowledge,
the church bells pealing, pealing

Punta Cana

The plane left the earth at 6am.
I looked at you, your eyes closed
your body tight and still and
I knew we were going into
a timeless place of just two,
but then I would breathe and be one again.

On the bus, the guide with a clotted
Spanish accent droned. I looked
at you and you did not see me yet.
Out the window, steam and palms
and green vines clutching green vines,
houses made of multicolored tin,
half-naked children in the dust and
dark men squatting by the curb
waiting for a truck with a day's work.

At the resort the brown people said *ola*
and brought us drinks in coconut shells.
You turned to see me and clutched me to you
as we went from the beach to the pool,
holding our books under straw-thatched
umbrellas with no watches or wallets.

Among coral reefs we held hands,
goggled faces in the strange silent world
of purple and yellow fish, then we sat
on the sifted sand where the shore
is pummeled by the ocean, letting our
bodies be pushed by the relentless movement
of the water, laughing like children.

Each day when the sun and wind pulled
all the energy from us we quietly climbed
the stairs to our room, washed the sand off
each other in a bubble bath, then touched
and rolled our bodies into one
for as long as we pleased.

Remainder

Put your fingers on me darling.
Don't give up just because
I'm not the girl I used to be,

not the girl who startled you
out of your lonely nights
and penthouse dreams.

We wallowed and swallowed
and rolled into one,
starting fires with our bellies,

shooting off sparks and electricity
with bedclothes and swollen energy.
We spent all our hopes on each other.

My humid eyes, your humid mouth
searched for something familiar
something visceral, anything intrinsic.

After a dozen vein-splitting years
I am not new, but I am more.
We are not then, but we are here.

There is a puddle of collective tears
at our feet and one remaining
in the palm of your hand.

The Desire

Let the desire
not to hurt each other burn white
in the bedroom window,
through the cracked glass it burns the brightest.

Let's not speak of hell
when we are in it;
my flesh is Satan to you
because it does not move like a puppet.

Let us not drink
more temporary wine
in the cockshut of the day,
in that futile repetition of sad refrains.

Let us boldly
face the light and admit
you are a gourmet meal
and I am not hungry today.

I am an arms-length away
and you are in a straightjacket.
I am lifting my shirt to show my scars
and you are wearing yours inside out.

When we are dead once again,
detached from our hope,
let us arise, resurrect into the light,
let us be born again.

When I return to the breeze
the green visions and waterfalls
wind chimes and pink petunias waving
I return to you.

Wife

Dusting pain off a silent surface,
sweeping boredom out of the door,
sleeping when she should be waking,
picking, picking crumbs up off the floor.

Fluffing his pillow to lie closer to hers,
setting, then resetting the table,
straightening piles of paperbacks to escape
the dreams that became a child's fable.

Doing a half a load of his laundry,
crying when the damn toast is burnt,
seeking shelter in her pretty bottle,
mopping a clean floor as if it weren't.

Dancing alone across the shiny wood,
falling, shattering a hopeless bone,
stitching and binding to make it all right,
wondering why she's dancing alone.

Sprucing up the agony of years
with a brand new yellow curtain,
calling him in her screaming, silent voice
but no one can hear her, she's certain.

Brushing the dog, someone to talk to,
another phone call says he'll be late,
dinner's on the table, teddy's on the rug,
she'll be sleeping alone or she'll wait.

Ashes of love sprinkled at her feet,
brush them off before anyone can see.
The house is perfect, the day is done,
maybe one day she'll set herself free.

To Have Love

In the midst of your hands on me
peace arrives.

The music stops and a nothingness
fills the void, a quietude,

your whisperings,
my clutching.

Where am I?
When did you come

to bring all these
senses to life?

And all this gratitude
coagulates in my brain

for what we have in this moment.
Then a sudden sadness

for someone who does not have
what we have,

does not know
what we know,

has never been loved
as we have loved.

On the Calm Side

Everything is on the calm side now,
lake water lapping the pebbled shore,

your softened eyes, my gentler mouth.
On the calm side speaking and not speaking

are the same, acknowledgments not needed
or craved, no disappointing turn of the head

as we look up at the abundant sky, the infinite
horizon, there is no straining to understand.

We have abandoned our world and there is nothing
in this place to resurrect what is dead.

My love is a tundra, vast and white .
On the calm side I feel it boil in my marrow.

It is still growing from the night I read
my poems to you—and you listened.

Where It Lived

It turns out
we've had it all wrong:
searching for our cravings
in what was not there,

looking for truth
in our small entitlements
like recalcitrant children
anchored in the past,

clinging to a hungry vision
with our spirits on a stretcher
we have casually paged off
the days like a magazine,

shredding the beautiful
admiring the awful.

But now we know:
in every silent day,
every glance not averted,
in every shuddering embrace,

in the poverty of sleepless nights
and red-eyed mornings
this is where the love lived,
stayed, thrived, survived.

There Is a Last Time for Everything

There was a last time my daughter
crawled across the brown shag carpet,
a last day my son sat on my lap
with a book, but I didn't write it down.
I didn't know I should.

A last time we played
in the green turtle sandbox and built
dream houses with miniature plastic wrap
pools and matchbox cars. Was it spring or fall?
How old were they?

Some firsts I meticulously recorded.
She rolled over on July 22.
He discovered his hands on March 8.
But no goodbyes are logged for days
we thought would never end.

At the end of the first marriage
there must have been a last kiss, a closing hug
or *I love you* before it turned to ashes
we couldn't unburn.
I have no memory of when those occurred.

My soul protects me from knowing
the last time I saw my friend
before she succumbed to cancerous cells,
how little I cared, how little I understood
what a singular moment it was.

There will come a night when you and I will
make love one last time.
You will move over my skin and lovingly enter me,
but we will not know
to cry in each other's arms.

III.

A mother is a thirsty woman drinking every last drop of the sea...

Grace

No one tells the new mother
that her baby is not hers to keep.

No one says—you will depreciate,
they will leave you, and your life

will become a disassembled puzzle
that you can never quite put back together,

even though you happily spent all your sick days
at home to hold a tissue to a runny nose,

even though you learned the art of placing coins
under a sleeping child's pillow,

even though you rocked that chair until
it wore a groove in the rug.

A mother is a thirsty woman drinking
every last drop of the sea,

but she can't hold the waves back
with the palm of her hand.

As she listens for their breathing sounds
in the night, as she tiptoes in to kiss their foreheads

and say her prayers, no one tells her
each day will vanish like snow in the sun.

And no one tells her it is possible
for her love to grow, that pride begets joy,

that every season of their lives will be a new,
unexpected and iridescent gift for her soul.

In the Waiting Room

a young couple
re-entered after their visit
with two feet of
black and white shadows
on a strip of paper.
They sat close in chairs,
heads together,
smiling, giggling,
glancing at each other
then back to the
sonogram images,
pointing at their favorites.

Then they sat quietly,
her hand on the
small mound
of her belly,
waiting,
as if they already loved
this baby,
as if they already knew
this child.

Mothers and Sons

There are few odes to mothers and sons
the briefest link of all, transient, evanescent
sometimes like a one-sided kiss.

Impish arms that locked your departing legs
slathered with tears, now are the ones
to do the recalcitrant leaving.

A boy went missing and you think
of the milk carton children. Then your search
ended in the curious, sonorous voice of a man,

still teaching you tolerance, often angered
at your prudently maternal words as they drop
out of your mouth like stones.

I see mothers and sons and I am obliged
not to say—delight in knowing him now
this is your time, your singular time

before God takes a hole-punch
to your mother-parts and you will be forced
to abdicate your inherent well-loved throne.

Yet he is the muse of the forthcoming,
the hope of the unborn, your redemption,
still pulsating, alive.

Bonfire

I see them together:
the connective tissues, the shared blood,
a counterpoint in firelight—and
something primal and holy in me turns.

Orange-yellow waves move over their glossy faces
and rotate like pinwheels in their eyes.
Her perfect tight-teeth smile and luminous hair.
His shoulders wide and strong, his great-grandfather's silhouette.

White sparks sprinkle upward between us.
My diaphragm expands and my ribs crack in this invisible triangle.
I am stretched like early-morning yoga,
depth perception altered in this stasis.

Leaves flutter in the heat, tree frogs sing, dogs chase
each other in and out of deep shadows. His voice,
her laughter brings stillness to my maternal island
and resurrection to what time cannot take from my soul.

The Rat

The animal creeping through the darkened
dining room was bigger than a mouse.

I was sitting in the dim light of a single lamp one room away,
children's voices floated from the drafty upstairs bedrooms,

cold air wafted through open crevices and thresholds
as news of the Gulf War babbled from the TV screen.

It came from beneath the window seat, a hole
in the rotten floorboards by the radiator

through the pitiful damaged latticework
that was meant to hide the rust and peeling paint.

As my head turned toward the unexpected motion
my heart said mouse, but my mind knew.

Stealthily it slithered to the remnant bird seeds
under the canary cage on the floor of the adjacent room.

The next night
up through the hole by the cellar laundry tub drain,

a trap, a loud snap
the children and I went down to look.

High Tide

Pelicans glide without losing formation
until one drops like a stone
into the sea for breakfast.

Dolphin fins appear and vanish,
massive swirls of salt water
gallop over the sand bank

and white foam encroaches on
our chairs, our books, our towels.
Water suddenly arrives

where it is not supposed to be,
on our self-proclaimed island,
our personal footage of beach.

My partner regresses to the age of eight,
his boogie board charges the menacing waves.
I rise from my reading

to see if he is in sight, all right,
then watch for the reappearance
of a stranger's child swallowed in surf.

Like the pelican eyeing his catch from above
I revert to being a mother
still with small children.

The Boneyard

Lonely tables and chairs suction
clusters of youth around them
as night comes, pulling them in
with brown bottles, tall glasses,
giant screens display frantic
human activity, blinking,
flashing, numbers, talking
mouths with no words,
bodies multiply like mutant cells,
disco music forces itself into
your ears and causes the bodies to bob
like blond-haired engine pistons.
Stalker-looking men tell you
your daughter is beautiful
and you want to take her home
but you can't because she's all
grown up. As the night goes on
you feel older and older,
but the drummer looks at you,
because you still love to dance,
and you know you're not dead yet.

Black Dress

The black dress had a singular sound and feel,
the *Audrey Hepburn dress*, the clerk said, and it was sold.

A wide décolleté draped with a wavy collar framed my cleavage.
It wrapped around my ribcage like a baby's swaddling,

pulled me in tight and feminine, the swishing skirt flared
to my calves with the urgency to twirl.

The rhinestones on the cuffs and swinging from my earlobes
matched the ones on my shoes and around my neck.

I opened my handbag to check on the two cotton handkerchiefs
I had been given, then I momentarily put my carefully made-up face

in my hands, but caught the tears before they marred my visage.
I moved down the aisle in a happy trance and sat down

to watch my son begin the life I had always dreamed for him.

Crawl Space

Wrestling with scarred cardboard and unwieldy
torn black bags, a miasma of dust particles
cloud up as I crawl through the space under
bedrooms, hallways, and slightly neater closets.

Years ago we hefted these remnants
of life into this crawl space with our younger arms
and abandoned it all to linger among mouse traps
and burgeoning broken technology.

Now we've cleared the empty cartons and
obsolete computer parts, a wheelchair,
an exercise bike, but trunks of treasures will remain
and grow old with us in this blended house.

Far back in the corner, pushed against a dank
cement wall I pull open brown flaps and find
her first plaid coat and matching hat, two snowsuits,
one pink, one green, his tiny baseball cap and jacket.

These will patiently wait in hiding
with their threads full of love, in the fabric
of well-lived childhoods and ineffable joy,
for someone to wear them again.

Diane Vogel Ferri retired from a career teaching children with special needs and now tutors adults seeking their high school equivalency degree. She graduated from Kent State University and holds an M.ED from Cleveland State University. Her previous chapbook, *Liquid Rubies*, was published by Pudding House Press. Her novel, *The Desire Path*, can be found on Amazon.

Diane has essays published by Cleveland State University, *Scene Magazine* and *Cleveland Christmas Memories* among others. Her poetry can be found in numerous journals including *Rubbertop Review, Plainsongs, Rockford Review,* and *Poet Lore*. She is a founding member of Literary Cleveland. Diane lives in Solon, Ohio with her husband. She has two wonderful adult children and three amazing grandchildren.

www.ingramcontent.com/pod-product-compliance
Lightning Source LLC
LaVergne TN
LVHW040117080426
835507LV00041B/1315